LIFTLOG

Diary and Guide for Strength Training
Second Edition

Nate Foster
Tim Houts

MASTERS PRESS

A Division of Howard W. Sams & Company

Published by Masters Press
A Division of Howard W. Sams & Company
2647 Waterfront Pkwy E. Dr, Suite 100, Indianapolis, IN 46214

LiftLog: Diary and Guide for Strength Training
Second Edition

First Masters Press edition published 1995
10 9 8 7 6 5 4 3 2 1

Printed in the United States of America.

Introduction and Preface
to the Second Edition

Introduction
Welcome to LiftLog.

We created LiftLog to be the ultimate training diary, with all the features strength trainers want. LiftLog offers more room to record your training than any diary available, plus concise and helpful training tips and workouts. Our full-color and black-and-white photos offer motivation and inspiration throughout the training year.

Note your training plateaus, valleys and peaks in the diary. Use the training information in the guide to bring you faster times and increased performance. And enjoy the photos featured throughout the book.

Preface to the Second Edition
First, thank you for making LiftLog so successful! Thanks to your great support and suggestions we've sold out of two printings and are now in our second edition. Second, here's a recap of LiftLog features:

Easy to use diary
You'll quickly appreciate our diary layout. You'll see a full week of training spread over facing pages. And, most importantly, you'll have plenty of room to write. LiftLog has more flexibility and room to write than any diary available.

112 days of diary pages
LiftLog offers the most number of pages to record your training, giving you 16 weeks of undated diary pages to record your training. And because they are undated, you can start and stop using the diary according to your schedule.

24 ALL NEW photographs
This edition features 24 ALL NEW full-color and black-and-white photographs to inspire and motivate throughout your training year. Enjoy them!

Good luck on a great season of training and racing.

Nate Foster and Tim Houts

About the Authors

Nate Foster

Stuart "Nate" Foster graduated from California State University at San Luis Obispo, where he was an NCAA All-American in Track and Field (Pole Vault and Decathlon).

He is certified by the American College of Sports Medicine and the National Strength and Conditioning Association of America as Personal Fitness Trainer and Sports Conditioning specialist. Nate currently owns and operates his own personal training company.

Tim Houts

Tim is the author of several fitness books. With more than 200,000 copies in print, the books cover a variety of sports and activities, including walking, running, cycling and weight lifting.

Tim began participating in competitive athletics at the age of nine, enjoying the camaraderie and competition of his local age-group swim team. He went on to play water polo at Stanford University and then took up running after graduation. He has run numerous 10K's and three marathons. His interest in running and swimming has also led him to compete in many triathlons.

Today, Tim enjoys mixing his workouts to include fitness walking, running, swimming, mountain biking, and competing in an occasional 10K or open-water swimming event.

Credits:

All photographs © 1995 Jim Amentler
Cover design by Suzanne Lincoln
Book design by Heidi Sandison

Table of Contents

Part I: TRAINING GUIDE

Part II: TRAINING DIARY

Warm-up and Stretching

Warm-up and cool-down

Always warm up before you workout to prevent injury and improve performance. And follow your workouts with cool-down exercises to help your body redistribute blood and carry out lactic acids. Remember, warming up and cooling down before and after each workout will not only prevent injury and improve performance, but also reduce muscle soreness and tightening.

Set your work-out schedule so that you always have at least 10 to 15 minutes to warm up at the beginning of your workout and 10 to 15 minutes to cool down at the end of your workout. Use activities that are continuous and that progress from a low to moderate intensity level as your warm-up and cool-down. These include running, stationary cycle, aerobics, and stair climber.

Stretching

Develop a solid stretching routine to incorporate with your warm-up and cool-down. Flexibility is important to improve your range of movement and enhance your body's overall performance. Choose stretching exercises that focus on major joint and connective tissue areas like shoulders, back, hips, knees, and ankles. Do all stretching movements slowly, gradually, and smoothly. Do not force, bounce, or strain to reach for positions of a stretch. Hold each stretching movement for a period of 15 to 30 seconds and then repeat. There are many exercises to stretch your body, but the following basics work the best:

Chest pull

Stand facing a door frame. Place your hands on the frame at shoulder level and walk through the doorway until tension is felt in the chest muscles. Or have a training partner behind you gently pull your arms behind your back in the same motion.

Side bends

Stand with feet shoulder-width apart. Extend one arm overhead and place the hand of your other arm on your hip. Bend towards the opposite side of the lifted arm and repeat on both sides.

Thigh stretch

Lie on your left side with your head resting on your left hand. Hold your right foot between the toes and ankle joint with your right hand and pull your heel towards your buttock. Repeat on the opposite side.

Alternate quad stretch

Stand facing a wall. Hold one foot between the toes and ankle joint as you bend your leg and gently pull the bottom of your foot towards your buttocks. Repeat on each side.

Hamstring and back stretch

Sit on the floor with your legs straight out in front of you, knees flat, toes pointed up, hands on your thighs. Now bend slowly towards your toes from the waist and exhale. Repeat this movement several times.

Move now to stretch your lower back. Lie flat on the floor with your legs extended and pull your right knee up to your chest with your hands. Repeat with the left knee and then with both knees.

Be specific with stretching exercises that pertain to your daily strength training program. Get into the habit of stretching. A flexible body is less prone to injury, runs smoother and recovers faster.

Nutrition

Good, sound nutrition is a critical element to any training program. If you want to build your best body possible, remember that nutrition is 60 percent of a strength training program's success. Maintain nutritional basics of a well-balanced diet composed of several servings from the four basic food groups. Well-balanced diets include: (1) carbohydrates, (2) proteins, (3) fats, and (4) vitamins and minerals.

Carbohydrates

Complex carbohydrates provide an excellent source of highly burnable "fuel" for strength training and can be a good source of protein, vitamins, and minerals. Normal dietary guidelines suggest you make carbohydrates 50-60% of daily caloric intake. Consider making carbohydrates a lower percentage of your caloric intake and proteins a higher percentage while strength training because of the need for extra proteins to rebuild muscle tissue.

Carbohydrates include: potatoes, rice, pasta, kasha, corn, peas, beans, and fruits and vegetables.

Proteins

Proteins are essential to build muscle tissue, ligaments, tendons, and bones. While normal dietary guidelines suggest you make proteins 15% of your caloric intake, consider making proteins a higher percentage while strength training. Use this formula to calculate daily protein needs: Consume one gram of protein for every 2.2 pounds of body weight. For example, a 150-pound person would need 68 grams of protein (150 ÷ 2.2 = 68.1). But remember that any excess protein will be converted into fat.

Choose proteins that are from lean sources such as turkey, skinless chicken, fish, and egg whites. Other proteins include meats, poultry, fish, cheese, beans and legumes, and whole wheat grains.

Fats

Fats in limited quantity are important to your body make-up. However, because of hidden fats in many foods, be aware of all fats you consume. Fats, ounce for ounce, contain twice the calories of proteins or carbohydrates. Limit your fat intake to 25-30% of caloric intake.

Use this formula when reading labels to determine fat percentage: Each gram of fat contains nine calories, so multiply the grams of fat by nine to find the total amount of calories derived from fat. Divide this number by the total number of calories to find the percentage of fat. Another rule of thumb is to look for products with less than 3 grams of fat per 100 calories (27% fat percentage). For example, a label showing 4.5 grams of fat and 150 calories is acceptable, while a label with 6 grams of fat and 150 calories is not.

3

Limit fats such as butter, cheese, vegetable oils, fried foods, peanut butter, and olives.

Vitamins and Minerals

A well-balanced diet is important to assure you get all the vitamins and minerals your body needs. Eat plenty of fruits and vegetables as a good source of vitamins and minerals. And consider taking supplements to offset any deficiencies you may have in your diet, which may be further depleted by your strength training efforts. Also evaluate taking amino acids for additional protein to help build lean tissue without the fat found in most protein sources.

Adjust your diet and supplements to what works best for you.

Review your diet

Track your diet for one week every six to nine months to see if your diet is made up of 55-60% carbohydrates, 15% proteins, and 25-30% fats. Adjust your diet accordingly based on your results. Consider tracking your diet more frequently if you find it far off your goals.

Defining Fitness and Setting Goals

Defining fitness as specifically as possible will make setting your goals easier. Think of fitness as a state of well-being consisting of optimum levels of strength, flexibility, weight control, and cardiovascular and aerobic capacities that help you participate fully in life.

Focus your goals

Remember this definition of fitness as you set your training goals and training routine. Take a moment to think about why you are training and what it means to you. Ask yourself if training is important to your health concerns. Is training specific to another sports activity you're involved in? Is it necessary for your career? Whatever the reason, understand what your doing and why.

Set realistic goals

Set your goals so they are realistic and reachable. Maximize your training time by noting goals in your diary and reviewing them each day before you train. Set short-term, mid-term, and long-term goals. Begin with short-term goals to achieve within your first 30 days. Add mid-term goals to reach in about 90 days. And set long-term goals that could run from 6 to 12 months. Remember that the more time you put into planning effective training programs, the more you'll get out of them. It takes dedication, desire, and determination to get results. Go for it and feel good about yourself!

Measure your progress

Before starting your strength training program, measure your body top to bottom. Record the information in the Measurements Chart included in the Training Guide every 30 days for 6 months. After 6 months note your key measurements only every 60 to 90 days. Review your overall progress periodically. Include your actual body weight before taking measurements.

Strength Training Basics

The human body begins to lose muscle tissue at a rate of one-half pound to more than a pound per year after the age of 30. Muscle tissue becomes both smaller and weaker due to lack of use as we age.

Find a strength training program to do at least 2 to 3 times per week to help you decrease body fat, increase muscle tissue, develop strength, and maintain a better overall appearance. Follow these basic principles of weight training:

Strength overload principle
When muscles are continually forced to lift, push, or pull a weight, they will respond by building size and strength to handle the demands. Set your workouts to overload each muscle group by doing enough sets and repetitions of each exercise to the point of muscle failure. Muscle failure is the point where the muscles cannot complete another lift, pull, or push.

Sets and repetitions
Sets are groupings of a series of repeated exercises or repetitions. Organize your workouts into sets and repetitions to get the most from your efforts. Adjust your sets and repetitions according to how heavy a weight is being lifted. Do fewer repetitions of heavier weights and more repetitions of lighter weights. Adjust the number of sets based on your level of fitness and the number of repetitions per set. Do sets and repetitions from one set of 15 repetitions, to five sets of 8 to 12 repetitions.

How much weight to use
Experiment with different weight levels to choose the right weight. Pick weight poundage so you can complete all the sets and repetitions asked for in your program. The weights should not be too heavy or too light. The weights are too heavy if you cannot complete the workout, and they are too light if you breeze through the workout too easily. Record your progress and review your Lift Log to help make adjustments. Lift Log can be the best tool you have to understand your improvements and lack of improvements.

Form is key
Remember the importance of form in your strength training programs. Form can be the difference between positive results and no results. Proper form will help prevent strength training injuries and help develop balance, coordination, and flexibility in the process. Ask your club's personal trainer for tips on your form.

Progression

Strive for progression with each strength training session weekly. That is, try to either increase (1) the repetitions or (2) the resistance (weights) in one or more exercises each session. If your program calls for 8 to 12 repetitions, for example, then anytime you can do more than 12 repetitions, increase your weights by about 5 percent. Beginners should strive to make a 5 percent increase in all exercises each week. Intermediate to advanced trainees should focus on a 5 percent increase in each exercise every 2 weeks or 10 percent per month. Remember that percentage increases will vary from exercise to exercise and individual to individual, but 5 percent of any exercise for any trainee should be a realistic goal. Remember that being progressive is the key to improving.

F.I.T.

Concentrate on three key factors to get the greatest benefits from your strength training exercises and workouts: (1) frequency, (2) intensity, and (3) time.

Frequency

Frequency is how often you train per week. Remember that you cannot store fitness. Strength train at least two or three days per week and up to five days if possible.

Intensity

Intensity is how hard you exert yourself during your strength training sessions. Find a level of intensity that increases your heart rate and breathing patterns. Adjust your levels of intensity to how you feel each training day. Remember to work hard, but not beyond your ability, training, or recovery level. Set your intensity pace by the clock based on :30 - :60 second rest intervals between sets for the upper body and :60 - :120 seconds for the lower body. Find the level of training intensity best for you. Begin with moderate workout intensity and increase as you improve.

Time

Time is how long your training sessions will take. As a beginner, spend about 30 minutes strength training and gradually increase the time over 30 days. Work toward a minimum of 45 minutes and build toward 60 - 90 minute workouts with short rest intervals.

Major Muscle Group Anatomy

Study the major muscle groups of the human body shown here to help you visualize how each strength training exercise helps. Understand which muscles are used in each exercise and their function. Select and focus your lifting exercises to isolate particular muscle groups.

Incorporate strength training that involves both anterior (back) and posterior (front) muscles so that balance is achieved to prevent injury and build better muscular form and symmetry. Use the following table and illustration to identify major muscle groups and key weight training exercises to use in your workouts.

Muscle	Best Exercises
1. Trapezius(Traps)	Shrugs, Upright Row, Cleans, Lateral Raises.
2. Deltoids (Delts)	Seated Press, Lateral Raises, Military Press, Dumbbell Press.
3. Pectorals (Pecs)	Bench Press, Incline Press, Dumbbell Press, Pushups, Pullovers.
4. Latissimus Dorsi (Lats)	Pull downs, seated rowing, dumbbell rowing, pull-ups, barbell rowing
5. Biceps	Barbell Curls, Dumbbell Curls, Cable Curls, Chinups.
6. Abdominal (Abs)	Sit-Ups, Knee-Ups, Leg Raises, Twists.
7. Forearms	Wrist Curls, Reverse Curls, Gripping Objects Isometrically.
8. Gluteals (Buttocks)	Squats, Lunges, Good Mornings.
9. Quadriceps (Quads)	Squats, Leg Press, Leg Extensions, Lunges.
10. Hamstrings (Hams)	Lunges, Leg Curls, Running Stairs, Hills, Sprinting.
11. Gastrocnemius (Calves)	Calf Raises, Calf Extensions, Seated Calf Raises.

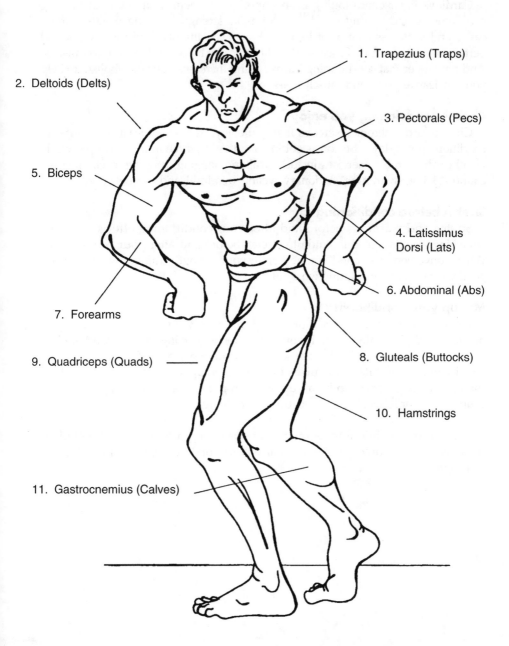

1. Trapezius (Traps)
2. Deltoids (Delts)
3. Pectorals (Pecs)
5. Biceps
4. Latissimus Dorsi (Lats)
6. Abdominal (Abs)
7. Forearms
8. Gluteals (Buttocks)
9. Quadriceps (Quads)
10. Hamstrings
11. Gastrocnemius (Calves)

Conditioning

Conditioning improves your strength training

Cardiovascular conditioning is an important element to all strength training programs. Conditioning will help you make strength training progress more easily and with less chance of injury. A well conditioned body will work and perform better because of increased ability to carry blood and oxygen to muscles. And remember that conditioning burns fat and increases your metabolism to help you stay lean as you build muscle mass.

Choose conditioning you enjoy

Choose cardio-aerobic exercises that you enjoy. Include at least 20 minutes of conditioning per day. Be consistent in conditioning three to five days per week. Good cardio-aerobic exercises include: walking, jogging, running, cycling, cross-country skiing, swimming, stationary cycling, treadmill, and racquet sports.

Stretch before conditioning

Stretch and warm up before and after your conditioning efforts. Use the stretching exercises in this guide to stretch before and after your conditioning. When convenient, use conditioning before your strength training workouts as a good warm-up for your lifting workout.

Mix up your conditioning

Incorporate different conditioning efforts into your training to keep you mentally and physically fresh. If you use stationary cycling as your conditioning, get on a mobile bike and enjoy the scenery as you work out. If you run for your conditioning, run different courses into the hills, up stairs, along the beach or shore, or through parks to break up your program. Or get on a pair of cross-country skies or roller skates to mix up your training.

Enjoy your conditioning as much as your strength training and include it consistently, and you'll get a body that will respond better, perform better and look better.

Organizing Your Workouts

Organize your workouts based on your fitness and strength training goals and the time you have available to train. Organize your workouts into either (1) a comprehensive workout that covers the whole body in less detail in one workout, or (2) an in-depth workout that covers parts of the body in greater detail in several workouts.

Organize by body part
The exercises listed below are organized by body part. For a comprehensive workout choose one to two exercises from each body part for a single workout to cover the whole body. For an in depth workout, choose three to five exercises from two or three body parts for focus on particular body parts; then alternate focus of body parts on alternating workout days.

Do sets and repetitions from 1 set of 15 repetitions to 5 sets of 8 to 12 repetitions.

Shoulders
Seated-Press with Barbells or Dumbbells
Press behind the neck with Barbells
Lateral raise with Dumbbells
Upright rowing with Barbells
Bent-over raise with Dumbbells

Chest
Bench Press with Barbells or Dumbbells
Incline Press with Barbells or Dumbbells
Bent-Arm Flies with Dumbbells
Decline Press with Dumbbells
Bent-Arm Pullovers with Dumbbells

Back
Lat Pull-down (Front, Rear)
Seated Rowing
Bent-Over Row with Barbells
Reverse Dumbbell Flies
Pull-ups wide or narrow grip
Alternate Dumbbell Rowing

Arms
Barbell Curls
Alternate Dumbbell Curls
Cable Curls
Triceps Press down on Cables
Triceps French Press with Dumbbells
Triceps Kickbacks with Dumbbells

Abdominal

Bent-Knee Crunches
Hanging Knee-ups from Bar
Leg Lifts lying on floor
Side bends with Dumbbells
Alternate Bent-Knee Crunches
Abdominal Cable Crunches

Upper Legs

Squats - Barbell or Dumbbell
Lunges
Leg Extensions
Leg Press
Hack Squats or Press

Lower Legs

Standing Calf Raise
Seated Calf Raise
Calf Raise with Leg Press
Jumping Rope
Stairmaster on your toes for the final 3 minutes of stepping

Be Alternative

Choose exercises that work opposing muscle groups and focus on major muscles that may be weaker than others. Alternate your training sessions so that you work the upper body hard and lower body easy, then the lower body hard and upper body easy. Try training your major muscles in groups.

Comprehensive example

Choose exercises that involve all major muscle groups starting from the top (shoulders) to the bottom (calves). Beginners do 1 set of 10 to 12 repetitions from each group; intermediates do 3 sets of 8 to 10 repetitions; and advanced complete 3 to 5 sets of 8, 10, 12, repetitions or 6, 8, 10, repetitions. Train your muscle groups in variation so that they are subject to different stimuli. Change your strength training routines every 3 to 4 months to maximize results.

In-Depth example

Do exercises for chest, back, biceps in one session; then shoulders, abdominal, and legs exercises in the next training session.

Sample Workouts

The following are examples of strength training programs for beginning, intermediate, and advanced workouts. The strength training programs include weekly sessions to from 1 to 12 weeks. Adjust them to fit your needs, goals, and fitness levels. Remember to complete all sets and repetitions in any given program. Concentrate on range of motion and form before being concerned about how heavy the weights you are lifting.

Program #1-Beginning
Weeks 1-4

Refer to this as a beginning program whether for use in a first time strength training program, or as a program to rebuild after a layoff. Always adjust your program to your fitness levels. Ask your club's personal trainer to give you tips on form and weight selection for each exercise.

Determine your maximum weight for each exercise. Use 20-30% of this weight as your training weight. Do each exercise 8-10 repetitions for one set. Do entire program three times per week, with a day off between efforts.

Increase the number of sets to two for each exercise after the second week. Increase to three sets after the third week.

Weeks 5-11

Refer to the following program as an intermediate program. Always adjust your program to your fitness levels. Ask your club's personal trainer to give you tips on form and weight selection for each exercise.

Determine your maximum weight for each exercise. Use 40% of this weight as your training weight. Do each exercise 12-15 repetitions per set. To make your workout more complete and intense, perform 30-45 seconds of aerobic activity between exercises. Activities include jogging, stationary cycling, and jump rope. Do entire program three times per week, with a day off between efforts.

Increase the number of sets to two for each exercise after the second week. Increase to three sets after the third week. Maintain at three sets.

Exercise	Sets	Repetitions
Leg press	1-3	12-15
Bench press	1-3	12-15
Leg curl	1-3	12-15
Pull down	1-3	12-15
Shoulder press	1-3	12-15
Sit ups	1-3	Maximum per set
Heel raise	1-3	Maximum per set
Curls	1-3	12-15
Triceps press	1-3	12-15

Program #2-Intermediate
Weeks 1-2

Choose one exercise per body part for the first two weeks. Do one set of fifteen repetitions per exercise. Ask your club's personal trainer to help you with your form for each exercise.

Weeks 3-5

Increase to two exercises per body part for weeks three through five. And increase the number of sets per exercise to two: one set of 15 repetitions and one set of 12. Increase the weight on the second set. Remember to adjust your program to your fitness level as it changes through your training cycle and be sure to complete all sets and repetitions in each exercise.

Weeks 6-12

Select three exercises per body part during weeks six through 12. Do all sets as listed below. Be aware of exercises that become easy and increase your weights as needed. But always complete all sets and repetitions before increasing weights.

Exercise	Sets	Repetitions
Back		
Wide-grip pull down	3	15-12-10
Seated row	3	15-12-10
T-bar row	3	15-12-10
Stiff-legged deadlift	3	15-12-10
Chest		
Bench press	3	15-12-10
Incline dumbbell press	3	15-12-10
Cable crossover	3	15-12-10
Dips	3	Maximum
Shoulders		
Military press	3	15-12-10
Lateral raise	3	15-12-10
Bent-over lateral	3	15-12-10
Legs		
Leg extension	4	16-14-12-10
Squat	4	16-14-12-10
Kack squat	4	16-14-12-10
Leg curl	4	16-14-12-10
Biceps		
Barbell curl	3	15-12-10
Preacher curl	3	15-12-10
Cable concentration curl	2	12-10

Triceps

Triceps press down	4	16-14-12-10
Close-grip bench press	3	15-12-10
Lying triceps extension	3	15-12-10
One-arm cable press down	3	15-12-10

Calves

Standing calf raise	2	20-15
Seated calf raise	2	20-15

Abdominal

Crunch	2	20-20
Rope crunch	2	20-20
Seated leg tuck	2	20-20

Program #3-Advanced

Use the following schedule and exercises as an advance workout. Use this program only after you've built the strength training and fitness levels to prevent injury. Select your weight levels so you can complete all sets and repetitions and adjust the program to your strength training and fitness levels. Weight levels should be 40-60% of your maximum. Use this program as a model to develop your own programs as you move through your training cycles.

Monday
Abdominal

	Sets	Repetitions
Crunches ✓	3-4	25-50
Leg raises *LOWER ABS*	3-4	20-25
Rotary torso	3-4	20-25

Chest

Bench press	3-4	10-12
Dumbbell incline press	3-4	10-12
One arm cable crossover	3-4	10-12
Dumbbell pullover	3-4	12-15

Back

Wide grip pull down	3-4	10-12
Seated lat row	3-4	10-12
Row machine ✓	3-4	10-12
One arm dumbbell	3-4	8-10

Conditioning

20 minutes cycling

Tuesday
Abdominal

Repeat Monday

15

Shoulders

Press behind neck	3-4	10-12-8-6
Steep shoulder press	3-4	8-10
Side arm lateral raise	3-4	8-10
Hammer raise	3-4	8-10

Biceps

Bent bar curl	3-4	8-10
Biceps machine	3-4	8-10
Scott curl	3-4	8-10

Triceps

Lying triceps extension	3-4	8-10
Triceps press machine	3-4	8-10
Pulley pushdown	3-4	8-10

Conditioning
20 minutes cycling

Wednesday
Abdominal
Repeat Monday

Legs

Leg extension	3-4	12-15
Leg curls	3-4	10-12
Leg press/squat	3-4	10-12
Toe raise	3-4	Maximum
Seated calf raise	3-4	Maximum
Stiff arm pullover	3-4	10-12

Conditioning
20 minutes cycling

Thursday
Repeat Monday

Friday
Repeat Tuesday

Saturday
Repeat Wednesday

Sunday
Day off

Program #4-Advanced

Use the following schedule and exercises as an advance workout. Use this program only after you've built the strength training and fitness levels to prevent injury. Select your weight levels so you can complete all sets and repetitions and adjust the program to your strength training and fitness levels. Use this program as a model to develop your own programs as you move through your training cycles.

Monday	Sets	Repetitions
Chest		
Bench press	2	15-15 (Warm up, light weight)
Bench press	3	8-10
Incline dumbbell press	3	8-10
Decline bench press	3	8-10
Cable cross over	3	8-10
Calves		
Leg press calf extension	2	15-15 (Warm up, light weight)
Leg press calf extension	3	8-10
Seated calf machine (toes out)	3	8-10
Seated calf machine (toes in)	3	8-10

Tuesday		
Shoulders		
Seated dumbbell press	2	15-15 (Warm up, light weight)
Seated dumbbell press	3	8-10
Wide grip upright rows	3	8-10
Seated side lateral	3	8-10
Bent over rear laterals	3	8-10
Barbell shrugs	3	8-10
Abdominal		
Machine crunches	3	15-20

Wednesday		
Back		
Wide grip pull down to chest	2	15-15 (Warm up, light weight)
Wide grip pull down to chest	3	8-10
Close grip pull down to chest	3	8-10
Seated row wide or close	3	8-10
Dumbbell row	3	8-10

Calves
Same as Monday

Thursday
Triceps

Close grip bench	2	15-15 (Warm up, light weight)
Close grip bench	3	8-10
Seated overhead dumbbell	3	8-10
Pushdowns	3	8-10
Kickbacks	3	8-10

Biceps

Standing barbell curl	2	15-15 (Warm up, light weight)
Standing barbell curl	3	8-10
Seated dumbbell curl	3	8-10
EZ Bar preacher bench	3	8-10
Concentration curl	3	8-10

Forearms

EZ Bar reverse grip	3	8-10
Wrist curl palms down	3	8-10

Friday
Legs

Squats	3	20 (Warm up, light weight)
Squats	3	10-15
Leg press	3	10-15
Leg extension	3	10-15
Leg curl	3	10-15
Straight leg dead lift	3	10-15

Abdominal

Same as Tuesday

Saturday

Day off

Sunday

Day off

Other Books to Read

This training guide offers tips and workouts to help you get more out of your strength training. Refer to these books for more in-depth discussions of other strength and fitness training topics:

Strength training

Baechle, Thomas R. and Grove, Barney R.: *Weight Training: Steps to Success*, Human Kinetics Publishers Inc.

Fahey, Thomas D. and Hutchinson, Gayle: *Weight Training for Women*, Mayfield Publishing Co.

Garhanmer, J.: *Sports Illustrated Strength Training*, Harper and Row

Oswitch, Gideon S.: *Myths and Truths in Fitness*, Wyatt Printing

Stone, M. and O'Bryant H.: *Weight Training: A Scientific Approach* , Burgess

Cross training

Doughty, Tom: *The Complete Book of Long Distance and Competitive Cycling*, Simon & Schuster

Fixx, James: *The Complete Book of Running*, Bantam Books

Maglischo, Ernest: *Swimming Faster*, Mayfield

Vaz, K.: *Cross Training, The Complete Book of Triathlon*, Avon Publishers

Nutrition

Brody, Jane: *Jane Brody's Good Food Book*, Bantam Books

Haas, Robert: *Eat to Win*, Rawson Associates

The Complete & Up-to-Date Fat Book, a guide to the fat, calories and fat percentages in your food, Avery Publishing

Periodicals

MuscleMag International, Canusa Products, Lincoln, Nebraska

Muscular Development, Advanced Research Press, Ronkonkoma, New York

Muscle and Fitness, Weider Publishing Inc., Woodland Hills, California

Men's Fitness, Weider Publishing Inc., Woodland Hills, California

Shape Magazine, Weider Publishing Inc., Woodland Hills, California

Getting More Out of Your Diary

Your personal coach

Use the Lift Log Training Diary as a tool to help you get the most out of your strength training. Lift Log's diary pages are simple and give you plenty of space and flexibility to decide what and how much information to record. The diary is like a personal coach to remind you of what you have or haven't done. It will keep you on track and keep you honest. It will show you why you're making progress and provide you with a wealth of information about your training.

Adjust to your needs

Adjust your notes according to your needs and training focus as you go through training cycles. The Lift Log diary allows you the flexibility to decide what training information is important to you to record. This information will change as your training programs change and you progress through your goals. For example, you may focus on your diet and body weight during early stages of a training cycle, and focus more on weights and repetitions later in a training cycle.

Be consistent

Be consistent in recording your training. Remember to record your body weight and measurements every 30 days. Also note how you feel on the days you train. Remember that the subjective data of how you feel is as important as the objective data of how much and how many you lift. Adjust your training diary to your needs, but try to keep it simple and take advantage of the space provided in the Lift Log to note your thoughts.

Use tracking charts

Use the tracking charts included in Lift Log to help you plan and track your improvements.

Measurements Chart

Use Measurements Chart to track improvements in your body measurements. Remember to measure yourself at the same time of day and at the same body points to get more accurate comparisons. Set goals for improvements. Track your measurements every 30 days for the first 6 months of your program and every 60 to 90 days afterwards. Review your training when you record your measurements to see why you're achieving the results you are. Adjust your program as needed.

Progression Chart

Use the Progression Chart to track your improvements in sets and repetitions for each exercise. Review your progress for each exercise in each body part group. Be sure you're not focusing on one body part excessively, while ignoring another body part. Enjoy entering these achievements and seeing your progress.

DAY WEDNESDAY DATE 7/7/93

EXERCISE/COMMENTS	SETS	REPS	WEIGHT

UPPER BODY PROGRAM:

WARM-UP: TREADMILL 14 min AT LEVEL ⑥

ABDOMINALS: 4 x 25   BOTH LOWER AND UPPER

BODY LIFTING: PULL-UPS: 4 x 10

BAR DIPS: 4 x 10

PUSH UPS: 4 x 15

① DB LATERAL RAISE: 3 x 10 @   15 lbs.

② BARBELL SEATED PRESS: 3 x 10 @ 85/95/85.

③ UPRIGHT ROWING: 3 x 12, 10, 8, @ 65/75/85.

④ DB INCLINE FLYS: 3 x 10 @ 25/30/25.

⑤ BENCH PRESS: 3 x 12, 10, 8, @ 135/175/185.

⑥ DB DECLINE PRESS: 3 x 12, 10, 8, @ 45/55/65.

⑦ PULL DOWNS (LATS): 3 x 10 @ 120/130/140.

⑧ SEATED ROWING: 3 x 10 @ 100/110/120.

⑨ DB ALT. ROWING: 3 x 10, 8, 6, @ 45, 55, 65.

⑩ BARBELL CURLS: 3 x MAX. REPS. @ ⑦⑤

⑪ DB ALT. CURLS: 3 x MAX. REPS. @ 30/35

⑫ TRICEP PUSHDOWN: 3 x MAX REPS. @ ⑦⓪

* COOL-DOWN: LIFECYCLE 12 min. @ RANDOM ⑤

CONDITIONING/NOTES FEELING STRONGER TODAY! UPPER BODY
WORKOUTS SHOW IMPROVEMENTS WITH MOST
LIFTS. NEED TO SPEND MORE TIME WITH
FLEXIBILITY DAILY! TRY TO INCREASE
CALORIES NEXT WEEK EACH DAY.
(STRETCH 15 min. TODAY)   TIME/DISTANCE

TOTAL WORKOUT
90 min.

Body Measurement Worksheet

	Start	30-Days	60-Days	90-Days	120-Days
Date					
Height					
Weight					
Neck					
Right upper arm					
Left upper arm					
Right forearm					
Left forearm					
Chest					
Waist					
Hips					
Right thigh					
Left thigh					
Right calf					
Left calf					

Goals/Notes: _____

_____

_____

_____

Progression Worksheet

	Start	30-Days	60-Days	90-Days	120-Days
	Sets/Rep/Wt.	Sets/Rep/Wt.	Sets/Rep/Wt.	Sets/Rep/Wt.	Sets/Rep/Wt.
Date:	_____	_____	_____	_____	_____

Exercise

_____	_____	_____	_____	_____	_____
_____	_____	_____	_____	_____	_____
_____	_____	_____	_____	_____	_____
_____	_____	_____	_____	_____	_____
_____	_____	_____	_____	_____	_____
_____	_____	_____	_____	_____	_____
_____	_____	_____	_____	_____	_____
_____	_____	_____	_____	_____	_____
_____	_____	_____	_____	_____	_____
_____	_____	_____	_____	_____	_____
_____	_____	_____	_____	_____	_____
_____	_____	_____	_____	_____	_____
_____	_____	_____	_____	_____	_____
_____	_____	_____	_____	_____	_____
_____	_____	_____	_____	_____	_____

Progression Worksheet

	Start	30-Days	60-Days	90-Days	120-Days
	Sets/Rep/Wt.	Sets/Rep/Wt.	Sets/Rep/Wt.	Sets/Rep/Wt.	Sets/Rep/Wt.
Date:	_____	_____	_____	_____	_____

Exercise

_____	_____	_____	_____	_____	_____
_____	_____	_____	_____	_____	_____
_____	_____	_____	_____	_____	_____
_____	_____	_____	_____	_____	_____
_____	_____	_____	_____	_____	_____
_____	_____	_____	_____	_____	_____
_____	_____	_____	_____	_____	_____
_____	_____	_____	_____	_____	_____
_____	_____	_____	_____	_____	_____
_____	_____	_____	_____	_____	_____
_____	_____	_____	_____	_____	_____
_____	_____	_____	_____	_____	_____
_____	_____	_____	_____	_____	_____
_____	_____	_____	_____	_____	_____
_____	_____	_____	_____	_____	_____

"Gray hair is God's graffiti."

— Bill Cosby

DAY

DATE

EXERCISE/COMMENTS	SETS	REPS	WEIGHT

CONDITIONING/NOTES

TIME/DISTANCE

DAY _____ DATE _____

EXERCISE/COMMENTS	SETS	REPS	WEIGHT

CONDITIONING/NOTES _____

_____

_____

_____

_____ **TIME/DISTANCE** [   ]

DAY _____

DATE _____

EXERCISE/COMMENTS	SETS	REPS	WEIGHT

CONDITIONING/NOTES _____

TIME/DISTANCE

DAY _____   DATE _____

EXERCISE/COMMENTS	SETS	REPS	WEIGHT

CONDITIONING/NOTES _____

TIME/DISTANCE

DAY _____   DATE _____

EXERCISE/COMMENTS	SETS	REPS	WEIGHT

CONDITIONING/NOTES _____

TIME/DISTANCE

DAY _____ DATE _____

EXERCISE/COMMENTS	SETS	REPS	WEIGHT

CONDITIONING/NOTES _____

_____

_____

_____

_____ TIME/DISTANCE

DAY _____   DATE _____

EXERCISE/COMMENTS	SETS	REPS	WEIGHT

CONDITIONING/NOTES _____

TIME/DISTANCE

DAY _____ DATE _____

EXERCISE/COMMENTS	SETS	REPS	WEIGHT

CONDITIONING/NOTES _____

TIME/DISTANCE

DAY _____   DATE _____

EXERCISE/COMMENTS	SETS	REPS	WEIGHT

CONDITIONING/NOTES _____

TIME/DISTANCE

DAY _____   DATE _____

EXERCISE/COMMENTS	SETS	REPS	WEIGHT

CONDITIONING/NOTES _____

_____

_____

_____   TIME/DISTANCE [   ]

DAY _____ DATE _____

EXERCISE/COMMENTS	SETS	REPS	WEIGHT

CONDITIONING/NOTES _____

_____ TIME/DISTANCE

DAY _____   DATE _____

EXERCISE/COMMENTS	SETS	REPS	WEIGHT

CONDITIONING/NOTES _____

_____

_____

_____

_____   TIME/DISTANCE

DAY _____ DATE _____

EXERCISE/COMMENTS	SETS	REPS	WEIGHT

CONDITIONING/NOTES _____

TIME/DISTANCE

DAY _____   DATE _____

EXERCISE/COMMENTS	SETS	REPS	WEIGHT

CONDITIONING/NOTES _____

TIME/DISTANCE

"A good man is always a beginner."

— *Martial*

"You are no bigger than the things that annoy you."

— *Jerry Bundsen*

DAY _____   DATE _____

EXERCISE/COMMENTS	SETS	REPS	WEIGHT

CONDITIONING/NOTES _____

_____

TIME/DISTANCE

DAY _____   DATE _____

EXERCISE/COMMENTS	SETS	REPS	WEIGHT

CONDITIONING/NOTES _____

TIME/DISTANCE

DAY _____   DATE _____

EXERCISE/COMMENTS	SETS	REPS	WEIGHT

CONDITIONING/NOTES _____

_____

_____

_____

_____   TIME/DISTANCE [_____]

DAY _____   DATE _____

EXERCISE/COMMENTS	SETS	REPS	WEIGHT

CONDITIONING/NOTES _____

TIME/DISTANCE

DAY

DATE

EXERCISE/COMMENTS	SETS	REPS	WEIGHT

CONDITIONING/NOTES

TIME/DISTANCE

DAY _____ DATE _____

EXERCISE/COMMENTS	SETS	REPS	WEIGHT

CONDITIONING/NOTES _____

TIME/DISTANCE

DAY _____ DATE _____

EXERCISE/COMMENTS	SETS	REPS	WEIGHT

CONDITIONING/NOTES _____

_____

_____

_____

TIME/DISTANCE _____

DAY _____   DATE _____

EXERCISE/COMMENTS	SETS	REPS	WEIGHT

CONDITIONING/NOTES _____

TIME/DISTANCE

DAY _____ DATE _____

EXERCISE/COMMENTS	SETS	REPS	WEIGHT

CONDITIONING/NOTES _____

_____

_____

_____

_____ TIME/DISTANCE

DAY _____ DATE _____

EXERCISE/COMMENTS	SETS	REPS	WEIGHT

CONDITIONING/NOTES _____

TIME/DISTANCE

DAY

DATE _____

EXERCISE/COMMENTS	SETS	REPS	WEIGHT

CONDITIONING/NOTES _____

TIME/DISTANCE

DAY _____ DATE _____

EXERCISE/COMMENTS	SETS	REPS	WEIGHT

CONDITIONING/NOTES _____

TIME/DISTANCE

DAY

DATE

EXERCISE/COMMENTS	SETS	REPS	WEIGHT

CONDITIONING/NOTES

TIME/DISTANCE

DAY

DATE

EXERCISE/COMMENTS	SETS	REPS	WEIGHT

CONDITIONING/NOTES

TIME/DISTANCE

"Fanaticism consists of redoubling your efforts when you have forgotten your aim."

— *George Santayana*

"The art of living is more like wrestling than dancing."

— *Marcus Aurelius*

DAY _____ DATE _____

EXERCISE/COMMENTS	SETS	REPS	WEIGHT

CONDITIONING/NOTES _____

_____

_____

_____ TIME/DISTANCE

DAY _____   DATE _____

EXERCISE/COMMENTS	SETS	REPS	WEIGHT

CONDITIONING/NOTES _____

_____

_____

_____

_____   TIME/DISTANCE

DAY _____ DATE _____

EXERCISE/COMMENTS	SETS	REPS	WEIGHT

CONDITIONING/NOTES _____

TIME/DISTANCE

DAY _____ DATE _____

EXERCISE/COMMENTS	SETS	REPS	WEIGHT

CONDITIONING/NOTES _____

TIME/DISTANCE

DAY _____ DATE _____

EXERCISE/COMMENTS	SETS	REPS	WEIGHT

CONDITIONING/NOTES _____

TIME/DISTANCE

DAY _____ DATE _____

EXERCISE/COMMENTS	SETS	REPS	WEIGHT

CONDITIONING/NOTES _____

TIME/DISTANCE

DAY _____ DATE _____

EXERCISE/COMMENTS	SETS	REPS	WEIGHT

CONDITIONING/NOTES _____

_____

_____

_____

_____ TIME/DISTANCE

DAY _____   DATE _____

EXERCISE/COMMENTS	SETS	REPS	WEIGHT

CONDITIONING/NOTES _____

TIME/DISTANCE

DAY _____   DATE _____

EXERCISE/COMMENTS	SETS	REPS	WEIGHT

CONDITIONING/NOTES _____

TIME/DISTANCE

DAY

DATE

EXERCISE/COMMENTS	SETS	REPS	WEIGHT

CONDITIONING/NOTES

TIME/DISTANCE

DAY

DATE

EXERCISE/COMMENTS	SETS	REPS	WEIGHT

CONDITIONING/NOTES

TIME/DISTANCE

DAY _____ DATE _____

EXERCISE/COMMENTS	SETS	REPS	WEIGHT

CONDITIONING/NOTES _____

_____

_____

_____

_____ TIME/DISTANCE [   ]

DAY _____ DATE _____

EXERCISE/COMMENTS	SETS	REPS	WEIGHT

CONDITIONING/NOTES _____

TIME/DISTANCE

DAY

DATE

EXERCISE/COMMENTS	SETS	REPS	WEIGHT

CONDITIONING/NOTES

TIME/DISTANCE

"I always turn to the sports pages
first, which record people's
accomplishments. The front page
has nothing but man's failures."

— *Chief Justice Earl Warren*

"God gives talent. Work transforms talent into genius."

— *Anna Pavlova*

DAY _____ DATE _____

EXERCISE/COMMENTS	SETS	REPS	WEIGHT

CONDITIONING/NOTES _____

TIME/DISTANCE

DAY

DATE

EXERCISE/COMMENTS **SETS** **REPS** **WEIGHT**

CONDITIONING/NOTES

TIME/DISTANCE

DAY _____   DATE _____

EXERCISE/COMMENTS	SETS	REPS	WEIGHT

CONDITIONING/NOTES _____

TIME/DISTANCE

DAY _____   DATE _____

EXERCISE/COMMENTS	SETS	REPS	WEIGHT

CONDITIONING/NOTES _____

_____

_____

_____

_____ TIME/DISTANCE [_____]

DAY

DATE

EXERCISE/COMMENTS	SETS	REPS	WEIGHT

CONDITIONING/NOTES

TIME/DISTANCE

DAY _____   DATE _____

EXERCISE/COMMENTS	SETS	REPS	WEIGHT

CONDITIONING/NOTES _____

_____

_____

_____

_____ TIME/DISTANCE

DAY _____ DATE _____

EXERCISE/COMMENTS	SETS	REPS	WEIGHT

CONDITIONING/NOTES _____

TIME/DISTANCE

DAY _____   DATE _____

EXERCISE/COMMENTS	SETS	REPS	WEIGHT

CONDITIONING/NOTES _____

_____

_____

_____

_____ TIME/DISTANCE [   ]

DAY

DATE

EXERCISE/COMMENTS	SETS	REPS	WEIGHT

CONDITIONING/NOTES

TIME/DISTANCE

DAY _____ DATE _____

EXERCISE/COMMENTS	SETS	REPS	WEIGHT

CONDITIONING/NOTES

TIME/DISTANCE

DAY _____ DATE _____

EXERCISE/COMMENTS	SETS	REPS	WEIGHT

CONDITIONING/NOTES _____

TIME/DISTANCE

DAY _____ DATE _____

EXERCISE/COMMENTS	SETS	REPS	WEIGHT

CONDITIONING/NOTES _____

_____

_____

_____

_____ TIME/DISTANCE [   ]

DAY

DATE

EXERCISE/COMMENTS	SETS	REPS	WEIGHT

CONDITIONING/NOTES

TIME/DISTANCE

DAY _____ DATE _____

EXERCISE/COMMENTS	SETS	REPS	WEIGHT

CONDITIONING/NOTES _____

_____

_____

_____

_____ TIME/DISTANCE _____

"But to look back all the time is boring. Excitement lies in tomorrow."

— *Natalia Makarova*

"I like being unconventional."

— Florence Griffith Joyner

DAY

DATE

EXERCISE/COMMENTS	SETS	REPS	WEIGHT

CONDITIONING/NOTES

TIME/DISTANCE

DAY _____ DATE _____

EXERCISE/COMMENTS	SETS	REPS	WEIGHT

CONDITIONING/NOTES _____

TIME/DISTANCE

DAY _____ DATE _____

EXERCISE/COMMENTS	SETS	REPS	WEIGHT

CONDITIONING/NOTES _____

TIME/DISTANCE

DAY _____ DATE _____

EXERCISE/COMMENTS	SETS	REPS	WEIGHT

CONDITIONING/NOTES _____

TIME/DISTANCE

DAY

DATE

EXERCISE/COMMENTS	SETS	REPS	WEIGHT

CONDITIONING/NOTES

TIME/DISTANCE

DAY _____   DATE _____

EXERCISE/COMMENTS	SETS	REPS	WEIGHT

CONDITIONING/NOTES _____

TIME/DISTANCE

DAY

DATE

EXERCISE/COMMENTS	SETS	REPS	WEIGHT

CONDITIONING/NOTES

TIME/DISTANCE

DAY _____ DATE _____

EXERCISE/COMMENTS	SETS	REPS	WEIGHT

CONDITIONING/NOTES _____

_____

_____

_____

_____ TIME/DISTANCE

DAY _____ DATE _____

EXERCISE/COMMENTS   **SETS**   **REPS**   **WEIGHT**

_____

_____

_____

_____

_____

_____

_____

_____

_____

_____

_____

_____

_____

_____

_____

_____

_____

_____

_____

_____

_____

_____

_____

_____

_____

_____

_____

CONDITIONING/NOTES _____

_____

_____

_____

_____ **TIME/DISTANCE**

DAY _____   DATE _____

EXERCISE/COMMENTS	SETS	REPS	WEIGHT

CONDITIONING/NOTES _____

_____

_____

_____

_____ **TIME/DISTANCE**

DAY _____   DATE _____

EXERCISE/COMMENTS	SETS	REPS	WEIGHT

CONDITIONING/NOTES _____

_____

_____

_____

_____   TIME/DISTANCE

DAY

DATE _____

EXERCISE/COMMENTS	SETS	REPS	WEIGHT

CONDITIONING/NOTES _____

_____

_____

_____

_____ **TIME/DISTANCE**

DAY

DATE

EXERCISE/COMMENTS	SETS	REPS	WEIGHT

CONDITIONING/NOTES

TIME/DISTANCE

DAY _____   DATE _____

EXERCISE/COMMENTS	SETS	REPS	WEIGHT

CONDITIONING/NOTES _____

TIME/DISTANCE

"If I'm too strong for some people, that's their problem"

— *Glenda Jackson*

"It's never too late to be what you might have been."

— George Eliot

DAY _____   DATE _____

EXERCISE/COMMENTS	SETS	REPS	WEIGHT

CONDITIONING/NOTES _____

_____

_____

_____

_____ TIME/DISTANCE

DAY _____   DATE _____

EXERCISE/COMMENTS	SETS	REPS	WEIGHT

CONDITIONING/NOTES _____

TIME/DISTANCE

DAY _____   DATE _____

EXERCISE/COMMENTS   **SETS**   **REPS**   **WEIGHT**

_____

_____

_____

_____

_____

_____

_____

_____

_____

_____

_____

_____

_____

_____

_____

_____

_____

_____

_____

_____

_____

_____

_____

_____

_____

CONDITIONING/NOTES _____

_____

_____

_____

_____   TIME/DISTANCE [   ]

DAY _____ DATE _____

EXERCISE/COMMENTS   **SETS**   **REPS**   **WEIGHT**

CONDITIONING/NOTES _____

TIME/DISTANCE

DAY _____ DATE _____

EXERCISE/COMMENTS	SETS	REPS	WEIGHT

CONDITIONING/NOTES _____

_____ TIME/DISTANCE [   ]

DAY _____   DATE _____

EXERCISE/COMMENTS	SETS	REPS	WEIGHT

CONDITIONING/NOTES _____

_____

_____

_____

_____   TIME/DISTANCE [   ]

DAY _____   DATE _____

EXERCISE/COMMENTS	SETS	REPS	WEIGHT

CONDITIONING/NOTES _____

TIME/DISTANCE

DAY

DATE

EXERCISE/COMMENTS   **SETS**   **REPS**   **WEIGHT**

CONDITIONING/NOTES

TIME/DISTANCE

DAY

DATE

EXERCISE/COMMENTS	SETS	REPS	WEIGHT

CONDITIONING/NOTES

TIME/DISTANCE

DAY

DATE

EXERCISE/COMMENTS	SETS	REPS	WEIGHT

CONDITIONING/NOTES

TIME/DISTANCE

DAY

DATE

EXERCISE/COMMENTS	SETS	REPS	WEIGHT

CONDITIONING/NOTES

TIME/DISTANCE

DAY _____ DATE _____

EXERCISE/COMMENTS	SETS	REPS	WEIGHT

CONDITIONING/NOTES _____

_____ TIME/DISTANCE

DAY _____   DATE _____

EXERCISE/COMMENTS   **SETS**   **REPS**   **WEIGHT**

_____

_____

_____

_____

_____

_____

_____

_____

_____

_____

_____

_____

_____

_____

_____

_____

_____

_____

_____

_____

_____

_____

_____

_____

_____

_____

_____

_____

CONDITIONING/NOTES _____

_____

_____

_____

_____

_____   **TIME/DISTANCE**

DAY

DATE

EXERCISE/COMMENTS	SETS	REPS	WEIGHT

CONDITIONING/NOTES

TIME/DISTANCE

"It's what you learn after you know it all that counts."

— *John Wooden*

"Life is too short to stuff a mushroom."

— Storm Jameson

DAY _____   DATE _____

EXERCISE/COMMENTS	SETS	REPS	WEIGHT

CONDITIONING/NOTES _____

TIME/DISTANCE

DAY

DATE

EXERCISE/COMMENTS	SETS	REPS	WEIGHT

CONDITIONING/NOTES

TIME/DISTANCE

DAY _____ DATE _____

EXERCISE/COMMENTS	SETS	REPS	WEIGHT

CONDITIONING/NOTES _____

TIME/DISTANCE _____

DAY

DATE

EXERCISE/COMMENTS	SETS	REPS	WEIGHT

CONDITIONING/NOTES

TIME/DISTANCE

DAY _____   DATE _____

EXERCISE/COMMENTS　　　　　　**SETS**　　　**REPS**　　　**WEIGHT**

CONDITIONING/NOTES _____

_____ TIME/DISTANCE

DAY _____ DATE _____

EXERCISE/COMMENTS	SETS	REPS	WEIGHT

CONDITIONING/NOTES _____

_____

_____

_____

_____ TIME/DISTANCE _____

DAY _____   DATE _____

EXERCISE/COMMENTS   **SETS**   **REPS**   **WEIGHT**

_____

_____

_____

_____

_____

_____

_____

_____

_____

_____

_____

_____

_____

_____

_____

_____

_____

_____

_____

_____

_____

_____

_____

_____

CONDITIONING/NOTES _____

_____

_____

_____

_____

                                        TIME/DISTANCE

DAY _____   DATE _____

EXERCISE/COMMENTS   **SETS**   **REPS**   **WEIGHT**

_____

_____

_____

_____

_____

_____

_____

_____

_____

_____

_____

_____

_____

_____

_____

_____

_____

_____

_____

_____

_____

_____

_____

_____

CONDITIONING/NOTES _____

_____

_____

_____

_____

_____   **TIME/DISTANCE** [_____]

DAY _____   DATE _____

EXERCISE/COMMENTS	SETS	REPS	WEIGHT

CONDITIONING/NOTES _____

_____

_____

_____

_____ TIME/DISTANCE [   ]

DAY _____   DATE _____

EXERCISE/COMMENTS	SETS	REPS	WEIGHT

CONDITIONING/NOTES _____

_____

_____

_____

_____ TIME/DISTANCE

DAY _____ DATE _____

EXERCISE/COMMENTS	SETS	REPS	WEIGHT

CONDITIONING/NOTES _____

_____

_____

_____

_____

TIME/DISTANCE [   ]

DAY _____   DATE _____

EXERCISE/COMMENTS	SETS	REPS	WEIGHT

CONDITIONING/NOTES _____

TIME/DISTANCE

DAY _____   DATE _____

EXERCISE/COMMENTS	SETS	REPS	WEIGHT

CONDITIONING/NOTES _____

TIME/DISTANCE

DAY _____ DATE _____

EXERCISE/COMMENTS	SETS	REPS	WEIGHT

CONDITIONING/NOTES _____

TIME/DISTANCE

"Luck is the residue of design."

— *Branch Rickey*

"One thing I do suffer from is over-confi-dence. It's something I'm working on."

— *George Foreman*

DAY _____   DATE _____

EXERCISE/COMMENTS	SETS	REPS	WEIGHT

CONDITIONING/NOTES _____

_____

_____

_____   TIME/DISTANCE

DAY _____ DATE _____

EXERCISE/COMMENTS	SETS	REPS	WEIGHT

CONDITIONING/NOTES _____

_____ TIME/DISTANCE [   ]

DAY _____ DATE _____

EXERCISE/COMMENTS	SETS	REPS	WEIGHT

CONDITIONING/NOTES _____

TIME/DISTANCE

DAY _____   DATE _____

EXERCISE/COMMENTS	SETS	REPS	WEIGHT

CONDITIONING/NOTES _____

_____

_____

_____

TIME/DISTANCE

DAY

DATE

EXERCISE/COMMENTS	SETS	REPS	WEIGHT

CONDITIONING/NOTES

TIME/DISTANCE

DAY _____   DATE _____

EXERCISE/COMMENTS	SETS	REPS	WEIGHT

CONDITIONING/NOTES _____

TIME/DISTANCE

DAY _____   DATE _____

EXERCISE/COMMENTS	SETS	REPS	WEIGHT

CONDITIONING/NOTES _____

_____

_____

_____

_____   TIME/DISTANCE

DAY _____ DATE _____

EXERCISE/COMMENTS	SETS	REPS	WEIGHT

CONDITIONING/NOTES _____

_____

_____

_____

_____ **TIME/DISTANCE**

DAY _____   DATE _____

EXERCISE/COMMENTS	SETS	REPS	WEIGHT

CONDITIONING/NOTES _____

TIME/DISTANCE

DAY _____   DATE _____

EXERCISE/COMMENTS	SETS	REPS	WEIGHT

CONDITIONING/NOTES _____

_____

_____

_____

_____ TIME/DISTANCE

DAY _____   DATE _____

EXERCISE/COMMENTS	SETS	REPS	WEIGHT

CONDITIONING/NOTES _____

TIME/DISTANCE

DAY _____   DATE _____

EXERCISE/COMMENTS	SETS	REPS	WEIGHT

CONDITIONING/NOTES _____

TIME/DISTANCE

DAY _____   DATE _____

EXERCISE/COMMENTS   **SETS**   **REPS**   **WEIGHT**

_____

_____

_____

_____

_____

_____

_____

_____

_____

_____

_____

_____

_____

_____

_____

_____

_____

_____

_____

_____

_____

_____

_____

_____

_____

_____

_____

_____

CONDITIONING/NOTES _____

_____

_____

_____

_____

                                              TIME/DISTANCE

DAY

DATE

EXERCISE/COMMENTS	SETS	REPS	WEIGHT

CONDITIONING/NOTES

TIME/DISTANCE

"I'd like to grow very old as slowly as possible."

— *Irene Mayer Selznick*